ANCIENT CITIES

POMPEII

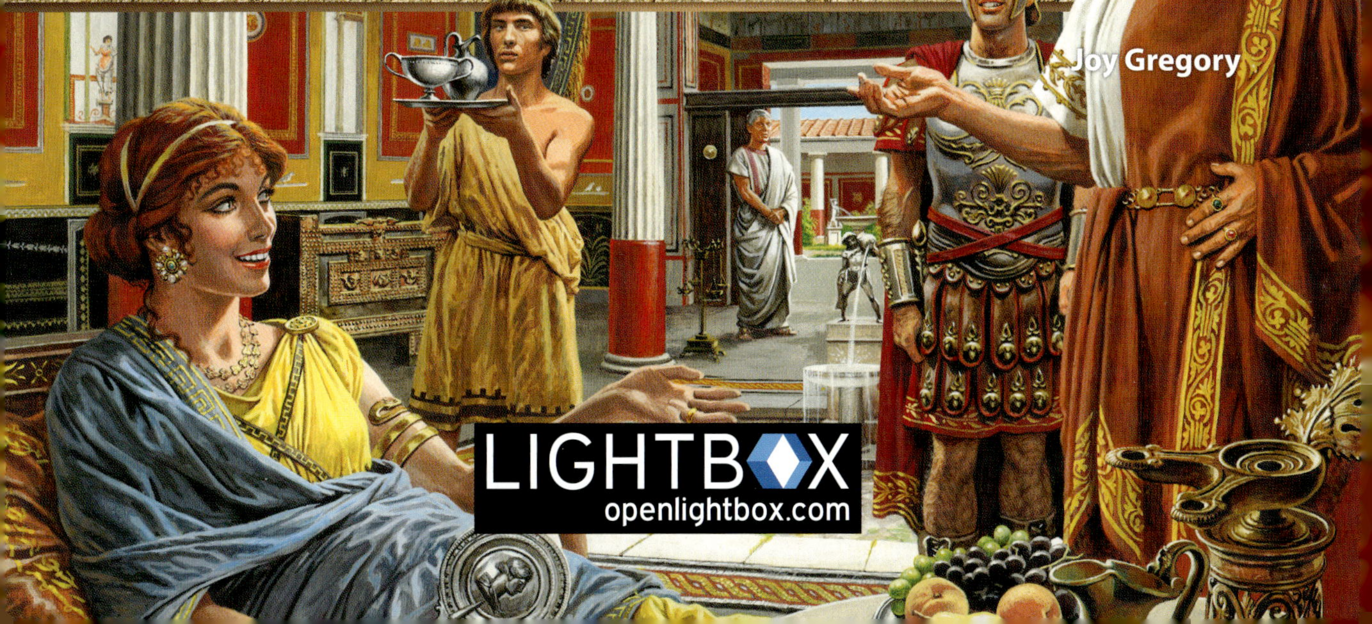

Joy Gregory

LIGHTBOX
openlightbox.com

LIGHTBOX

Go to
www.openlightbox.com
and enter this book's
unique code.

ACCESS CODE

LBXR5476

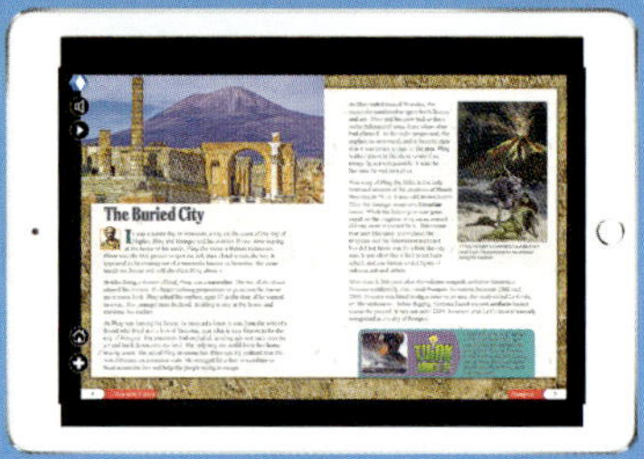

Lightbox is an all-inclusive digital solution for the teaching and learning of curriculum topics in an original, groundbreaking way. Lightbox is based on National Curriculum Standards.

LIGHTBOX SUPPLEMENTARY RESOURCES

SHARE
Share titles within your Learning Management System (LMS) or Library Circulation System

CURRICULUM
Find national and state curriculum correlations

CITATION
Create bibliographical references following APA, CMOS, and MLA styles

STANDARD FEATURES OF LIGHTBOX

AUDIO High-quality narration using text-to-speech system

ACTIVITIES Printable PDFs that can be emailed and graded

SLIDESHOWS Pictorial overviews of key concepts

VIDEOS Embedded high-definition video clips

WEBLINKS Curated links to external, child-safe resources

TRANSPARENCIES Step-by-step layering of maps, diagrams, charts, and timelines

INTERACTIVE MAPS Interactive maps and aerial satellite imagery

QUIZZES Ten multiple-choice questions that are automatically graded and emailed for teacher assessment

KEY WORDS Matching key concepts to their definitions

This title is part of our Lightbox digital subscription

Lightbox Grades 6–8 Subscription
ISBN 978-1-5105-6068-0

Access hundreds of Lightbox titles with our digital subscription. Sign up for a **FREE** subscription trial at **www.openlightbox.com/trial**

The digital components of this book are guaranteed to stay active for at least five years from the date of publication.

ANCIENT    CITIES

POMPEII

CONTENTS

The Buried City

It was a sunny day in Misenum, a city on the coast of the Bay of Naples. Pliny the Younger and his mother, Plinia, were staying at the home of his uncle, Pliny the Elder, a Roman statesman. Plinia was the first person to spot the tall, dark cloud across the bay. It appeared to be coming out of a mountain known as Vesuvius. She came inside the house and told the elder Pliny about it.

Besides being a Roman official, Pliny was a **naturalist**. The site of the cloud piqued his interest. He began making preparations to go across the bay to get a closer look. Pliny asked his nephew, aged 17 at the time, if he wanted to come. The younger man declined, deciding to stay at the house and continue his studies.

As Pliny was leaving the house, he received a letter. It was from the wife of a friend who lived at the foot of Vesuvius, near what is now known to be the city of Pompeii. The mountain had exploded, sending ash and rock into the air and back down over the land. The only way she could leave her home was by water. She asked Pliny to rescue her. Pliny quickly realized that this was a disaster on a massive scale. He arranged for a fleet of warships to head across the bay and help the people trying to escape.

As Pliny sailed toward Vesuvius, the mountain continued to spew forth flames and ash. Pliny and his crew had to dock miles (kilometers) away from where they had planned. As the night progressed, the explosions continued, and it became clear that it was unsafe to stay in the area. Pliny walked down to the shore to see if an escape by sea was possible. It was the last time he was seen alive.

Pliny the Elder is believed to have died from breathing in the poisonous fumes released during the eruption.

This story of Pliny the Elder is the only firsthand account of the eruption of Mount Vesuvius in 79 AD. It was told in two letters Pliny the Younger wrote to a **historian** friend. While the letters provided great detail on the eruption, they never named the city most impacted by it. This meant that later historians knew about the eruption and the destruction it caused, but did not know exactly where the city was. It was clear that it had never been rebuilt and was buried under layers of volcanic ash and debris.

More than 1,500 years after the volcano erupted, architect Domenico Fontana accidentally discovered Pompeii. Sometime between 1592 and 1600, Fontana was hired to dig a canal in an area the locals called La Civita, or "the settlement." While digging, Fontana found ancient **artifacts** buried under the ground. It was not until 1763, however, that La Civita was formally recognized as the city of Pompeii.

THINK ABOUT IT!

Imagine that you are living in Pompeii when the nearby mountain begins to spew smoke, ash, and stone onto the city. You and your family escape to safety. Later, you learn that a young man wrote two letters about what he saw that day. Why might you want to read those letters?

Who Were the Pompeiians?

Pompeii was settled by a people known as the Oscans between 900 and 800 BC. The Oscans were native to what is now southern Italy. They controlled a region known as Campania, which included Pompeii. Initially a village, Pompeii grew over time. Its proximity to the Tyrrhenian Sea helped it evolve into a busy port city.

In the centuries that followed, Pompeii's strategic position led several groups to battle for control of the city. The Samnites, who spoke Oscan, and the Romans were two of the main combatants. In 310 BC, a fleet of Roman soldiers arrived in Pompeii by sea and took control of the city. With Roman soldiers living in the city, Pompeii **allied** with Rome against other conquerors.

Roman Religion

Rome's influence over the people of Pompeii also extended into the area of religion. The Romans followed a polytheistic religion, meaning that they worshiped multiple gods. These divine beings were believed to control the Romans' daily lives. Under Roman law, certain gods and goddesses had to be worshiped on a regular basis. Temples were built in their honor. Most people had **shrines** in their homes.

Ongoing struggles between Romans and their allies in the area, collectively known as Italians, led to an open conflict called the Social War. When the war ended in 89 BC, the Romans and Italians united their territories under Rome. Pompeii's residents became citizens of Rome as a result.

The city became heavily influenced by Roman culture. Under Roman law, Latin became the official language. Buildings were constructed in the Roman style. Rome's leaders monitored the city's local government, overruling decisions that did not agree with their views. When a riot broke out after a **gladiator** fight in 59 AD, Rome's emperor banned these tournaments in Pompeii and replaced the local politicians with people of his own.

By granting the Italians citizenship at the end of the Social War, the Romans had the level of commitment needed to begin developing a professional army. In the years that followed, the Roman army would conquer much of Europe on behalf of the Roman Empire.

Marcus Attilius

Marcus Attilius was a gladiator who fought in the **amphitheater** at Pompeii. Like other Pompeiian gladiators, he probably lived in the House of Gladiators. This was a building where gladiators lived and trained. Marcus Attilius is known because of **graffiti** found in the city. Graffiti drawings show that Attilius carried a large shield. He wore a helmet with a curved brim. While most gladiators were slaves, Attilius was not. It is believed that he may have been an ex-soldier who needed money. The drawings indicate that Attilius won the first two fights of his career and that both of his opponents lived. The first was against Hilarus, an experienced gladiator who had already fought 14 times before he faced Marcus Attilius.

Where Is Pompeii?

Pompeii is located on the southwest coast of modern-day Italy, a country in Europe. It is southeast of both Rome, Italy's capital city, and Naples, the capital of Campania, now an Italian region. Pompeii was built close to where the Sarno River meets the Bay of Naples, in the Tyrrhenian Sea. While Pompeii was once a coastal city, it is now about 2,300 feet (700 meters) inland, due mainly to the volcanic activity of Mount Vesuvius. Built on a flat piece of land, the city is situated approximately 5 miles (8 km) from the base of Mount Vesuvius. It originally covered an area of about 1 square mile (3 square km).

A Mount Vesuvius

Mount Vesuvius is the only active volcano in mainland Europe. The mountain is 4,203 feet (1,281 m) high. Its base is 30 miles (48 km) wide. Mount Vesuvius last erupted in 1944.

B Tyrrhenian Sea

The Tyrrhenian Sea covers an area of about 106,000 square miles (275,000 sq. km). It is the third-largest body of water in the Mediterranean Sea. The Tyrrhenian Sea is part of several trade routes, linking several countries.

C Sarno River

The Sarno River is 15 miles (24 km) long and drains an area covering 276 square miles (715 sq. km). Much of that land is used by agricultural and industrial businesses. Today, the Sarno is considered one of the most polluted rivers in Europe.

D Herculaneum

Herculaneum was a community 5 miles (8 km) southeast of Naples. Built on a steep slope of Mount Vesuvius, it was also buried when the volcano erupted. More than 4,000 people lived there at the time. Many were wealthy people who had summer homes in Herculaneum. Scientists believe that many of Herculaneum's residents died while trying to escape.

Pompeii Location Map

A Growing Settlement

Pompeii's early settlers likely saw the potential in building a community along the coast. Access to the sea allowed them to catch fish and other seafood. This not only provided them with food, but also led to the development of a fishing industry, with much of the catch **exported** to people farther inland. Some of that fish, for example, was sold to people who lived up the Sarno River.

The land around Pompeii was also well suited to agriculture. Local farmers grew olives, figs, and nuts to sell at markets in Pompeii. Others sold field crops, such as onions, cabbage, and wheat. Some of this food was exported by sea to other cities and countries. Ships that carried away locally grown food also **imported** exotic spices, foods, and silk.

Over time, the seaside city became one of the most important trading ports on the Bay of Naples. The success of the fishing and agriculture industries attracted many new residents, who came in search of work and other opportunities in the area. The arrival of more people brought the construction of new homes, public buildings, and roads. Large temples and entertainment venues were also built.

Today, crops continue to be grown in Pompeii, with vineyards found at various points in and around the site.

To serve the growing population, some Pompeiians opened value-added businesses, where they turned local products into higher-value items. Some made olive oil and *garum*, a type of fermented fish sauce that was popular on Roman tables. The city also developed a fullery industry. These businesses bought raw wool from the area's farmers and turned it into cloth. Winemakers, bakers, and jewelers were just some of the other business owners who set up shops in the city.

Food shops were one of the most common types of businesses lining Pompeii's streets. However, businesses selling pots and pans, home décor, and cloth were also common.

By the year of the eruption, approximately 12,000 people lived in Pompeii. Another 10,000 people lived on the land around the city. Many of these people were farmers. However, the warm climate and beautiful views of Mount Vesuvius made this area a popular destination for wealthy people from Rome, who owned many vacation homes in the region.

Roman vacationers contributed greatly to Pompeii's prosperity. They often came to town, where they spent their money at shops, restaurants, and entertainment venues.

Building Pompeii

The Romans are known to have been very good builders. They constructed buildings and **infrastructure** that have survived centuries of use. Roman **engineers** applied their knowledge to building and maintaining structures in Pompeii. In 62 AD, parts of the city were damaged by a powerful earthquake. Reconstruction was still in progress when Mount Vesuvius erupted. The debris collapsed some roofs, but most of the city remained standing.

Roman Concrete

Most structures in ancient Roman cities, including Pompeii, were built using stones that were cut and pieced together. These stones were held in place by Roman concrete. This type of concrete was more durable than modern concrete. When sprayed with water, it could even repair its own cracks. Scientists are trying to learn how the product was made. They know it includes a specific mix of stones, limestone, and water. It also contains volcanic ash collected from a site near Naples.

100 x How much longer Roman concrete lasts compared to modern-day concrete

EPIC FACTS

The **Aqua Augusta** was at least **87 miles (140 km)** in length. At the time of its construction, it was the **largest Roman aqueduct**.

Lifting a **2.5-ton (2.3-metric ton)** stone block would take **50 people**. Using a **treadwheel crane** would require only **3**.

Aqua Augusta

Pompeii's supply of fresh water came from a Roman **aqueduct** known as Aqua Augusta. The aqueduct was made up mostly of underground canals. The canals connected several cities along the Bay of Naples. Typically made of concrete, the canals were engineered with a downward slope. This allowed the system to use gravity to move the water. Pipes fed the water to homes and businesses, as well as to public baths and fountains.

60 miles The distance fresh water traveled underground to reach Pompeii (97 km)

Street Smarts

The streets of Pompeii were built to manage the constant flow of water. Large stones on the surface of streets were set in a slight arch so that water would flow to the sides. High stone curbs lined the sides. They directed water through the city, protecting businesses and homes from floods. Stepping stones were set at regular intervals. People used the stones to cross the street without getting their feet wet.

12 inches The height of the curbs that lined the streets of Pompeii (30 centimeters)

Getting a Lift

Putting heavy rocks and blocks of concrete in place required much effort. The Romans invented equipment to make this job easier. The treadwheel crane relied on both human power and simple machines to lift heavy materials. The crane had a large wheel on it, which was connected to a central shaft, or axle. Workers would walk inside the wheel, causing the central shaft to turn. The shaft controlled a **pulley** that lifted an object up or down. The workers would walk one way to lift the object and the other to lower it.

= 6,600 pounds The weight that a treadwheel crane could lift (3,000 kilograms)

A City Takes Form

It took hundreds of years to build the city of Pompeii. Its construction and design show centuries of Roman influence. Like other great cities in ancient Rome, Pompeii's neighborhoods and markets were built on a grid system. This means most of its streets and canals followed patterns made of straight lines and right angles.

The oldest homes in Pompeii were built in the 4th century BC. The ruins show that Pompeii neighborhoods were not divided by wealth. Small and mid-sized homes were built beside the massive homes of the wealthy. Many homes also had commercial businesses in the same building. The business owners lived in the back of the building or on upper floors.

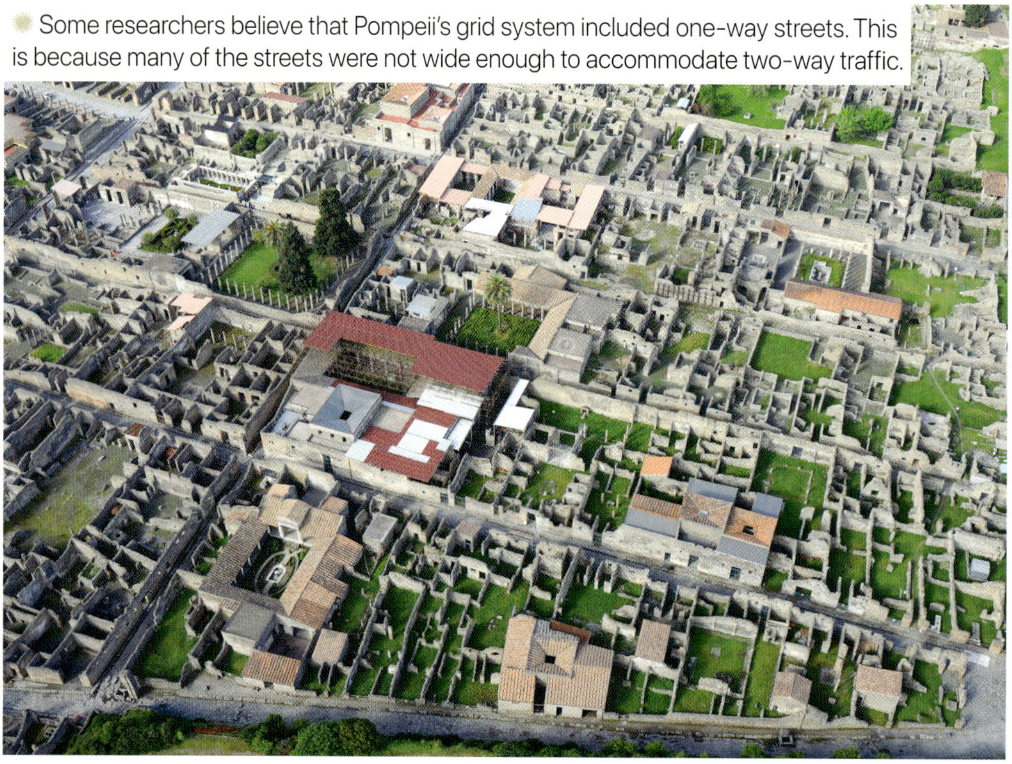

Some researchers believe that Pompeii's grid system included one-way streets. This is because many of the streets were not wide enough to accommodate two-way traffic.

The city had three main public bath houses. Used by the rich and poor, the public baths were free or charged a small fee. Some public baths included a swimming pool and exercise area. The private homes owned by wealthy Pompeiians had their own baths. However, as public baths gave people a place to socialize, many affluent Pompeiians still went to the bath houses.

Roman design also influenced where public buildings were placed. Public baths were located in different parts of the city. Major markets and entertainment areas were also built in different areas. This helped with crowd control. People rushing to the market to buy bread were not surrounded by fans going to watch a gladiator fight. **Archaeologists** have also found at least 40 ancient public fountains. These provided free water to the people of Pompeii.

Religion played an important role in people's lives. This is why temples and street shrines were located throughout Pompeii. Their accessibility allowed people to take a few minutes to worship when on their way to other places. As Pompeii's population grew, more temples and public buildings were added.

Pompeii's houses were often built close to each other and, in some cases, on top of each other, in apartment-style buildings called *insulae*.

More than 50 street shrines and altars can be found on the streets of Pompeii.

Inside Pompeii

Pompeii displays the world's most complete look at life in ancient Rome. Thousands of buildings and artifacts remain where they stood when Mount Vesuvius erupted. From grand mansions and markets to public fountains and kitchen tools, Pompeii is an archaeological treasure chest.

1

Forum

The rectangular Forum was the center of daily life in Pompeii. Government buildings were located here. Local and imported goods were traded at the large public market. People did their business and then went to worship at the temples nearby.

2

Forum Baths

The Forum Baths were near the Forum. Like other public baths, the space was divided into men's and women's bathing areas. Each section had three main rooms. This allowed bathers to bathe in warm, hot, or cold water.

3

Amphitheater

The amphitheater in Pompeii is one of the largest stone amphitheaters ever discovered. Built in 70 BC, its circular design could seat up to 20,000 people. People came here to watch live entertainment. Animals were often part of the shows staged here.

4

Theaters

Pompeii's two main theaters were located west of the amphitheater. Built in the Greek style, their stages faced a semi-circular seating area. The stone benches were built into a hill. The largest theater held about 5,000 spectators. The theaters hosted musical performances and plays.

5

House of the Faun

The House of the Faun was one of the largest residences in Pompeii. The home covered 32,000 square feet (3,000 sq. m), which is about an entire city block. It included four dining rooms and two large gardens. Construction began on the site of a preexisting building in about 180 BC, with rooms added over time.

6

Temple of Apollo

The Temple of Apollo is one of the oldest temples in Pompeii. Parts of the building were built more than 2,500 years ago. A bronze statue called Apollo with Bow is one of the temple's main highlights. The statue seen today is a copy of the original, which is now on display at a museum in Naples.

The People of Pompeii

Pompeii's residents lived in a prosperous community. However, the city's residents were not all equal. The city's social structure was based on freedom and wealth. The system divided residents into three main categories. At the top level, people were part of the freeborn elite. Under that, they were freedmen or slaves. Freeborn women were in a class that hovered between freedmen and slaves.

Social Hierarchy

Power played a key role in Pompeii's social structure. The people with the most power also had the most freedom and money. They were at the top of the social pyramid. The people with the least power were at the bottom of this structure.

Elites

Pompeii's elite class was made up of three different groups. All were freeborn, meaning that they had never been slaves. The senatorial elite were wealthy freeborn men. Many lived in Rome and had summer homes in Pompeii. Even so, their wealth and stature gave them much influence within the city. They were known to help fund new buildings and other city projects. The local elite ranked slightly lower in power. These Pompeiians lived in the city year-round. Most were wealthy businesspeople and landowners. Many were involved with local politics. Some worked for the Roman government. Other freeborn men also belonged to the elite class. They held jobs ranging from traders and shopkeepers to artisans and farmers.

Freedmen

Freedmen were also called *liberti* or *libertini*. These former slaves could earn their freedman status in two ways. Some were granted freedom by their owners. Others bought their freedom with money they earned. Many *libertini* worked in trades and did jobs the elite did not want to do. Some also worked for businesses owned by elites. Freedmen could earn their way to higher social status. However, no matter how much success they achieved, they were never allowed to vote.

Freeborn Women

Freeborn women in Pompeii could inherit and own property. They could run businesses and build personal wealth. Most of the trades were also open to women, but their freedom was not complete. Business decisions often required the support of a woman's father or husband. A fatherless and unmarried woman was required to have a male legal guardian make business decisions on her behalf. As with freedmen, freeborn women were also not allowed to vote.

Slaves

More than 30 percent of Pompeii's population were slaves. Under Roman law, slaves were the property of the people who owned them. Many of these men, women, and children were born to slaves who lived in Pompeii. Others were brought to Pompeii from other lands or captured in Roman battles. Some were sold into slavery by their families, who used the money to pay bills. Pompeii's slaves were assigned mostly to hard labor and domestic work. However, some slaves also worked as tutors and scribes, and could perform other tasks that required specific skills.

THINK ABOUT IT!

Slavery was part of life in Pompeii. Even the middle class kept slaves to keep their homes and businesses running. Slaves in Pompeii led difficult lives. They did the hardest and dirtiest jobs on farms and in businesses. They had no say in public life. How did this system contribute to life in Pompeii? Who benefited the most? Why might Pompeii's elite have thought this was a fair system?

A Day in the Life

Pompeii was at its busiest during the morning hours between 8:00 and 9:30 AM, also known as the *hora quarta*. This is when most people were out of the house running errands and meeting with friends.

As with other cities in ancient Rome, daily life in Pompeii started early. People did not have electricity, so they rose when the Sun came up. Their days probably started before 5:00 AM. The first meal of the day was simple. Breakfast for many people was cheese and bread. By 9:00 AM, the streets of Pompeii bustled with shopkeepers and shoppers. Traders brought goods into the city on wooden carts.

At noon, when the Sun was highest, people took a break to eat lunch. They likely ate bread, fish, and fruit. The public baths were busy in the early afternoon. Most people, wealthy or poor, bathed every day. Slaves probably washed themselves in the homes where they worked. Some were allowed to use certain areas of the public bath houses. Politicians and businesspeople often held meetings at the bath houses.

EPIC FACTS

Even after **hundreds of years** of digging, only about **two-thirds** of **Pompeii** has been uncovered.

More than **30 bakeries** have been found in the **ruins** of **Pompeii** so far.

Public shows at the amphitheater and theaters were held in the morning or afternoon. It was too dark to stage a show at night. People needed enough sunlight to get safely to and from the event.

Entertainment at Pompeii's theaters was varied. While plays were common, the theaters also hosted music festivals and mime performances.

The children of Pompeii were educated according to their social status. Wealthier families had private tutors. Some people sent their boys to public schools. The poorest families taught their children the skills they needed to work. Girls learned how to do household chores.

Many homes in Pompeii did not have a kitchen, so people bought their food at restaurants. Other homes had an open hearth in the kitchen, but no oven. These residents bought their bread and cake from bakeries. Some bakeries **excavated** at Pompeii were very well preserved. Archaeologists have found ovens, bread-making tools, and loaves of bread.

Most people ate their supper meal at about 5:00 PM. Historians believe Pompeiians ate fish, chicken, fruit, and nuts for supper. Archaeologists found evidence of this at Pompeii and Herculaneum. Since homes and streets were dark when the Sun went down, Pompeiians went to bed early.

Many of Pompeii's bakeries sold their products directly to customers. Others, however, acted as wholesalers. The bakery on Vicolo Storto, for instance, does not have an attached shop, and so it is believed to have sold baked goods to other businesses, such as food shops and street vendors.

The Eruption of Vesuvius

At about noon on August 24, 79 AD, Mount Vesuvius began to erupt, shooting a combination of ash, stone, and poisonous gases into the air. The event came as a surprise to Pompeiians. No one knew that the nearby mountain had been created by a volcanic eruption nearly 200,000 years earlier. They were unaware that it was a volcano that had been **dormant** for centuries. The people of Pompeii did not even have a word for volcano. To them, Vesuvius was just a mountain.

Residents of the city did not know what to do. When the eruption began, some people took shelter in their homes and businesses. Thousands of others began to flee. They could see where the debris was coming from, and they ran in the opposite direction.

Vesuvius did not stop erupting until the morning of the following day. Scientists believe that most of the people who stayed were killed by the extreme heat the volcano generated. Others died after breathing in the clouds of poisonous air. As Pliny the Younger mentioned in his letters, the eruption also caused earthquakes. Some people lost their lives when the earthquakes caused buildings and walls to collapse on top of them.

It is estimated that approximately 1.5 million tons (1.34 million metric tons) of debris were spewed into the air every second during Vesuvius's eruption.

At the time, Titus was the emperor of Rome. He knew the city would be looted by treasure hunters. To counter this criminal activity, he sent guards to prevent theft and vandalism. The guards were not needed. The natural disaster had completely buried the site. Ash and stone protected Pompeii from thieves, vandals, and the weather.

Approximately 2,000 Pompeiians were killed by the eruption of Mount Vesuvius. Close to 20,000 people survived. No one is sure what happened to the survivors. With the city completely buried, they could no longer live in Pompeii. In 79 AD, Pompeii was populated by locals, foreigners, migrants, and slaves. Most of these people did not have family names. There were no records of where they went. The majority likely settled in other communities on the southwest coast of Italy.

Today, restoration experts work to return Pompeii to as much of its original state as possible. Repainting wall art and repairing floor tiles is just part of the work involved.

Pompeii Today

Pompeii offers an extraordinary look at the people of ancient Rome. Visitors can walk through ancient homes, businesses, and temples. They can see paintings and large pieces of mosaic art. Many tourists marvel at the graffiti messages scrawled on walls and tombs. They can also see plaster **casts** of some of the people and animals that died as a result of the eruption.

In 1997, Pompeii was declared to be a UNESCO World Heritage Site. UNESCO is the United Nations Educational, Scientific and Cultural Organization. The World Heritage Site title is given to places that UNESCO wants to protect for future generations. Some of the sites are in remote locations. However, Pompeii is quite easy to visit. In fact, it is at risk because of the sheer number of people who want to walk through its ruins.

Approximately 110 acres (44.5 hectares) of Pompeii is open to visitors. In 2021, the site also opened its museum, the Antiquarium of Pompeii, which allows people to see many of the artifacts found during excavations of the city.

Years of excavation have exposed Pompeii's ruins to damage from the Sun, wind, and rain. In 2010, part of the House of Gladiators collapsed after heavy rains.

Pompeii is one of the busiest tourist attractions in the world. More than 2 million people visit the site every year. Many of them arrive on cruise ships or as part of regional tours. All of this foot traffic harms the ancient site. Roads and sidewalks are **eroding** due to the high number of people walking through the city. Wall **frescoes** have been damaged when visitors brush up against them. Some tourists have even vandalized the site by removing pieces of buildings to take home as souvenirs.

Local, state, and UN officials work together to preserve Pompeii. Recent discoveries at the site show there is still much to learn about the people who lived and died in this city. In 2019, excavators discovered a restaurant similar to modern-day fast-food outlet. A few years later, archaeologists unearthed the remains of a room believed to have served as quarters for slaves. Scientists view this as a major discovery, offering new information about the living conditions of slaves in the days of ancient Rome. As new technology is developed, it is possible that scientists will learn even more about this ancient city.

THINK ABOUT IT!

Some experts have argued that the excavation of Pompeii should stop. They feel that it is more important to put money toward preserving the areas already excavated than to try to uncover more. Still, the digging continues, with more sections of the city being unearthed. Which action do you think is best? Why is it better than the other option?

Timeline of Pompeii

The ruins of Pompeii reveal much information about the people who lived and died there close to 2,000 years ago. However, the city's real story begins long before Mount Vesuvius erupted.

900–800 BC

Pompeii is settled by the Oscans. The city is built on land created by earlier eruptions of Mount Vesuvius.

89

The Social War between Romans and Italians ends with the union of the two civilizations. The people of Pompeii receive Roman citizenship.

POMPEII

900 BC

310

89

70

310

Rome sends its soldiers to live in Pompeii. Pompeii remains self-governed but is now protected by the larger nation.

70

The amphitheater of Pompeii is built. The stone structure attracts large crowds to watch events that include circus shows and gladiator battles.

62 AD

On February 5, a powerful earthquake destroys many buildings in Pompeii. Rome sends workers to help with reconstruction.

1592–1600

Architect Domenico Fontana discovers Pompeii when digging a canal in the region. Workers uncover ancient artifacts, and locals begin to call the area La Civita.

2021

A four-wheeled bridal chariot is discovered at Pompeii under 13 feet (4 m) of volcanic ash. It is adorned with silver and bronze decorations.

62 AD | 79 | 1594–1600 | 1748 | 2021 | 2023

79

Mount Vesuvius takes Pompeii by surprise when it erupts on August 24. The eruption lasts for two days, kills thousands of people, and buries the city.

1748

King Charles VII of Naples sends people to La Civita to excavate the site. The king wants statues and objects to display. However, the haphazard excavation causes great damage to the site.

2023

Archaeologists find the skeletons of two men under a collapsed wall. Scientists believe that this confirms Pliny the Younger's account that earthquakes occurred after the eruption of Mount Vesuvius.

Make a Plaster Cast

In 1860, Giuseppe Fiorelli was chosen to direct a large-scale excavation of Pompeii. A professor of archaeology at the University of Naples, Fiorelli invented a technique that used plaster casts to make **replicas** of artifacts. These replicas allowed people to learn about Pompeii, its residents, and the impact of the eruption. Try making your own plaster cast by doing the activity below.

You will need

- One rubber glove
- Plaster of Paris
- Water
- Measuring cup
- Stir stick
- Bucket or bowl
- Cardboard tube long enough to hold rubber glove
- Scissors
- A human helper

Steps

1. Place the rubber glove into the cardboard tube. Stretch the top of the glove over the cylinder. Let the fingers and thumb hang inside the container.

2. Mix the plaster according to the instructions that come with the package. Remove any lumps.

3. Pour the plaster into the glove. Gently tap the cylinder on the table. This will help the plaster fill the glove. Smooth the top part of the plaster. Set the container where it will not be disturbed. Let the plaster set for 48 hours.

4. When the plaster is dry, carefully remove the glove from the cylinder. Use the scissors to cut off the glove.

5. Examine your cast.

Research Activity

The burial of Pompeii was quick and complete. Survivors could not find their own homes and businesses. Even looters were foiled. Over time, interest in the site decreased. No one knew where to look for artifacts. That changed when a few items were found accidentally hundreds of years later.

Write an opinion paper about why the excavation and preservation of Pompeii matters to the world at large. Look for information that strengthens your argument. Visit your school or local library and conduct some online research. Find examples of what we have learned from the archaeological site at Pompeii. Use those examples to support your position. The following questions will guide your research.

1. How has the excavation of Pompeii improved or increased our knowledge of the ancient Romans? Note examples of interesting facts you have learned about life in ancient Rome.
2. The science of archaeology has changed greatly since Pompeii was first discovered. What new technologies have been used to study the ruins of the ancient city? What additional knowledge have scientists gained about Pompeii as a result of using them? Why is this information useful?
3. Where can people who cannot visit Pompeii see some of the artifacts uncovered there? Why is it important for people in other countries to know about Pompeii? Besides the artifacts themselves, what is lost when people loot an ancient ruin?

Test Your Knowledge

Test your knowledge of Pompeii by answering these quiz questions.

1

What is the name of the volcano that erupted and buried Pompeii?

2

In what year did the volcano bury Pompeii?

3

How many spectators could the amphitheater of Pompeii hold?

4

Approximately what percent of the people who lived in Pompeii were slaves?

5

How old was Pliny the Younger when he watched Mount Vesuvius destroy Pompeii?

6

In what year did archaeologists uncover a bridal chariot at Pompeii?

7

In what year did part of the House of Gladiators collapse after heavy rains?

8

What was the name of the other city buried by the eruption of Mount Vesuvius?

ANSWERS: 1. Mount Vesuvius **2.** 79 AD **3.** 20,000 **4.** 30 percent **5.** 17 **6.** 2021 **7.** 2010 **8.** Herculaneum

Words to Know

allied: organizations, countries, or people that work together

amphitheater: an open-air venue with a circular or oval shape that was used for entertainment performances and sports

aqueduct: a structure for carrying water across land

archaeologists: people who study the objects and buildings left behind by past human activity

artifacts: objects made by humans

casts: copies made in plaster of another three-dimensional form

dormant: inactive or asleep

engineers: people who design or build engines, machines, or public works

eroding: wearing down

excavated: dug in the ground to look for objects that have been buried for a long time

exported: moved goods out of a country

frescoes: pictures made by painting on wet plaster on a wall or ceiling

gladiator: a person engaged in a public fight to entertain the people who lived in ancient Rome

graffiti: the words and pictures drawn on public surfaces, such as walls, that is usually not authorized

historian: someone who uses written sources and archaeological findings to study the past

imported: to bring goods into a country

infrastructure: the system of public works built and operated by governments

naturalist: a person who studies plants and animals

pulley: a simple machine made of a wheel with a rim that a cord or rope fits around

replicas: exact copies

shrines: places for worship

Index

LIGHTBOX

SUPPLEMENTARY RESOURCES

Click on the plus icon found in the bottom left corner of each spread to open additional teacher resources.

- Download and print the book's quizzes and activities
- Access curriculum correlations
- Explore additional web applications that enhance the Lightbox experience

LIGHTBOX DIGITAL TITLES

Packed full of integrated media

VIDEOS

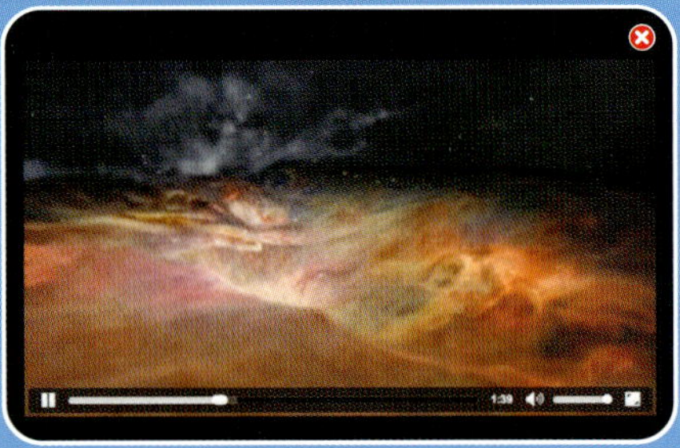

INTERACTIVE MAPS

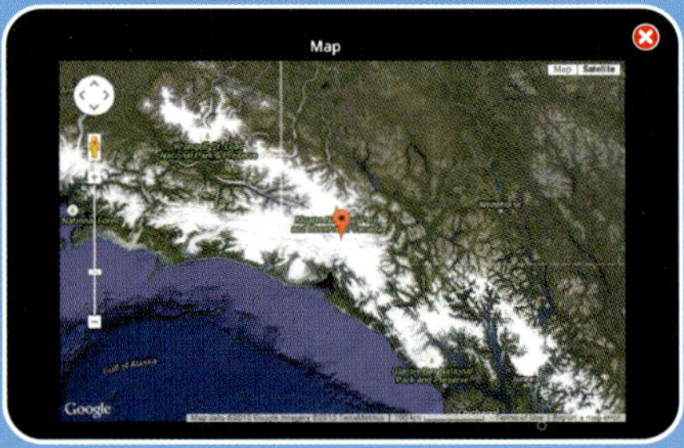

WEBLINKS

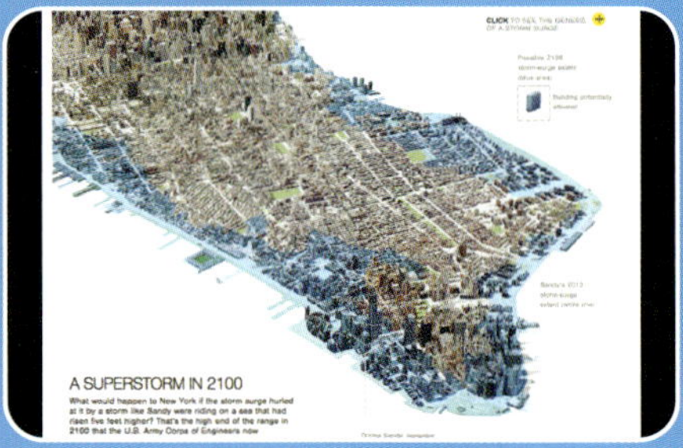

SLIDESHOWS

QUIZZES

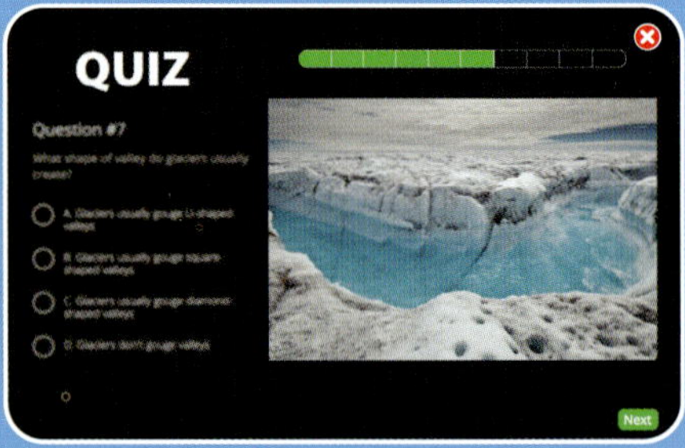

OPTIMIZED FOR

- ✓ TABLETS
- ✓ SMART BOARDS
- ✓ COMPUTERS
- ✓ AND MUCH MORE!

Published by Lightbox Learning Inc.
276 5th Avenue, Suite 704 #917
New York, NY 10001
Website: www.openlightbox.com

Project Coordinator Heather Kissock
Designer Terry Paulhus
Layout Mandy Christiansen

Library of Congress Cataloging-in-Publication Data

Names: Gregory, Joy, author.
Title: Pompeii / Joy Gregory.
Description: New York, NY : Lightbox Learning Inc., 2024. | Series: Ancient cities | Includes index. | Audience: Grades 4-6
Identifiers: LCCN 2023038156 | ISBN 9781510565180 (library binding) | ISBN 9781510580411 (ebook)
Subjects: LCSH: Pompeii (Extinct city)--Juvenile literature.
Classification: LCC DG70.P7 G735 2024 | DDC 937/.72568--dc23/eng/20230908
LC record available at https://lccn.loc.gov/2023038156

Printed in Stevens Point, Wisconsin, United States of America
1 2 3 4 5 6 7 8 9 0 27 26 25 24 23

112023
111222

Photo Credits
Every reasonable effort has been made to trace ownership and to obtain permission to reprint copyright material. The publisher would be pleased to have any errors or omissions brought to its attention so that they may be corrected in subsequent printings. The publisher acknowledges Getty Images, Alamy, Bridgeman Images, Newscom, Shutterstock, and Wikimedia Commons as its primary image suppliers for this title.